THE
REAL
CHRISTIAN

And Those Who Wear Masks

DR. STEPHEN SWIHART

DR. STEPHEN SWIHART
WWW.MAKINGDISCIPLES.US

CONTENTS

Part One
The Prevalence of Deception

1 Satan Wears a Mask   7
2 Satan's Helpers Wear Masks   17

Part Two
The Protection of Discernment

3 The Real Christian No Longer
   Follows the World   25
4 The Real Christian No Longer
   Follows Satan   32
5 The Real Christian No Longer
   Follows His Sinful Nature   41
6 The Real Christian is
   Born Again   47
7 The Real Christian Has a
   Testimony   57

*Additional Resources to
Help You Grow*   63

About the Author   64

Part One
The Prevalence of Deception

- *How will the donated money be used?* The funds would go to train youth in leadership skills so they can make the world a better place.

- *What do you believe about Jesus and salvation?* His answers reflected his own beliefs, not the positions of his so-called church. The "church" he represented had no interest in promoting Jesus or salvation.

- *Where do you live?* He didn't live in the community, but in a city a dozen states away from the restaurant.

The whole experience had the word "SCAM" written all over it, but I saw it as an opportunity instead. So I told the young fellow I would give him a donation if he would do three things:

1. Come back in twenty minutes, after we've finished eating.

2. Read a small book I will give him for FREE. (The book I wanted him to read is called "The Only Way to Heaven — Really!" It's a 50-page evangelistic book I wrote.)

3. Go to my website after you read my book and tell me you've read all of it. Also, ask me any questions you might have.

He agreed. When he came back, I took him to my car, gave him my book and a $20 donation. I also said something like this:

Benjamin, I've got to tell you, you are not part of a true church. When you lay down tonight, I want you start reading my book. I want you think about Jesus and why he came to earth — he wants to forgive you of your sins and give you a new life! Please promise me you will take Jesus and my book seriously.

He nodded his head, smiled, said, "God bless you." He walked away. Moments later, my wife and I prayed for Benjamin that God would open his eyes and enable him to recognize the deception in his heart and his so-called church!

In this small book I want to help you recognize *real* Christians (and even *real* churches), but first, I want to begin with a few eye-opening facts dealing with the prevalence of deception. You will probably be surprised to learn how often you and I have actually encountered imitation religious individuals and institutions. They are literally everywhere! But they are not quickly spotted because both Satan and his servants wear masks!

SATAN WEARS A MASK

Satan disguises himself as an angel of light
(2 Corinthians 11:14b).

You probably wouldn't recognize Satan if he were standing just a couple feet in front of your face. I wouldn't either. Why? Because he disguises himself; he wears a mask. In fact, outwardly he looks quite handsome and harmless . . . even spiritual . . . *until you get to know him.* Then, you realize he isn't what you thought. He isn't a good person. He isn't your friend. Instead, he's depraved to the core; he's your worst possible enemy! Satan has only one interest in spending time with you; he wants to deceive you; he wants to manipulate your mind; and he wants you to trust him . . . all of the way to hell!

In the very first appearance of Satan in the Bible we discover he is incredibly clever and deceptive in his practices. In order to trick and trap Eve, he employed three distinct strategies; today, he continues to use these same time-tested scams. Here's the account from Genesis 3. See if you can detect his three lethal tactics.

> *The serpent was the shrewdest of all the wild animals the Lord God had made. One day he asked the woman, "Did God really say you must not eat the fruit from any of the trees in the garden?"*

> *"Of course we may eat fruit from the trees in the garden," the woman replied. "It's only the fruit from the tree in the middle of the garden that we are not allowed to eat. God said, 'You must not eat it or even touch it; if you do, you will die.'"*

> *"You won't die!" the serpent replied to the woman. "God knows that your eyes will be opened as soon as you eat it, and you will be like God, knowing both good and evil."*

> *The woman was convinced (Gen. 3:1-6a).*

In this passage you witness the devil's modus operandi — his method for engaging in people's lives, usually without them even recognizing his operation! Observe how he approaches Eve.

- First, he works through "the shrewdest" (the smartest and least likely) creature in the Garden of Eden to be a trouble maker. There were no red flags or alarms going off here. Everything appeared innocent and harmless. WARNING: *Satan won't approach you as Satan!* Instead, he will come to you through a family member, a friend, a teacher/professor, a pastor, an entertainer, a politician, a successful businessman, or something similar. He will use someone or something you trust in order to trick you!

- Second, he uses ordinary speech to activate your thoughts and opinions. WARNING: *He wants you to have an open mind; he wants you to think for yourself.*

  A long time ago a friend taught me this profound statement. It would be time well spent if you committed it to memory: *Whoever controls you from your eyebrows up will also control you from your eye-brows down!*

  Visualize that sentence in your mind. Say it to yourself. Repeat it three or four times a day throughout the next week; do it until you can't forget it — *Whoever controls me from my eyebrows up will also control me from my eyebrows down!*

Now, let's get very specific; let's look at the three ways Satan will tamper with your mind in order to get you to think the way he wants you to think.

1. He will put doubts in your mind about the integrity and authority of God's Word.

This is the critical first step. Commit it to memory: Satan will always twist what God has said; he wants you to *doubt* God's Word!

Notice the first words out of the devil's mouth: "Did God really say . . ." On the surface, it sounds harmless. The serpent seems only to be looking for clarification. But in reality, he is putting a subtle question in Eve's mind. Read the sentence again. This time, emphasize the key word: "Did God *really* say . . ." In other words, "Eve, are you *certain* God said this? That doesn't sound quite right. Why would God say something like that? I have my doubts that God would ever make that kind of statement."

WARNING: This is where Satan always begins: *he finds a way to cast doubts about the inspiration, the accuracy, and the supremacy of God's Word.* He will not accept what God says; he will invariably make God's Word seem unreasonable or false. He used this approach in the Garden, and he continuously uses it today as well.

According to the apostle Paul, *All Scripture is inspired by God and is useful to teach us what is true and to make us realize what is wrong in our lives. It corrects us when we are wrong and teaches us to do what is right*

(2 Tim. 3:16). In other words, the Bible is our supernatural Manual for Life. It teaches us the truth about God's reality, His love, and His will. The devil knows this is true, but he is God's enemy and he doesn't want you to believe the Bible, so in one way or another he will ask you the same thing he asked Eve: "Did God *really* say . . .?" In short, Satan will do everything he can to get you to question the authenticity and authority of God's Word in the Holy Bible! **When that happens, the battle line is clearly drawn: will we believe God's Word, or will we believe the devil's progressive deception?**

Right this very moment, you need to evaluate your own opinions about the trustworthiness of the Bible. Do you believe the messages in this Book; do you accept them as inspired and authoritative? Do you believe the Scriptures represent the truth, the whole truth and nothing but the truth on everything it addresses? Or, do you regard the Bible as merely a religious text?

Please excuse me, but I must be frank: *If you doubt the inspiration and absolute authority of the Bible, then Satan has control of your mind this very minute!*

Let me help you. If you are uncertain about the Bible's accuracy, then I urge you to read my small book (just 48 pages) called "5 Reasons Why You Can Trust the Bible." If you will do that, you will be able to *detect* and *defeat* the devil in his tracks! You will be able to tell him boldly and confidently that you will not put up with his lies! This is what you need to do: Go to my website and download this pdf book for FREE; it is my pleasure to give you this eye-opening defense of the Bible's unrivaled inspiration. Go to www.MakingDisciples.us. Do it right away!

2. *He will attempt to get you to deny the teachings in the Bible, especially about Divine judgment.*

When Eve explained to Satan how God would judge anyone who ate from the forbidden tree, the devil immediately voiced his disagreement. *"You won't die!" the serpent replied to the woman.*

This is one of the devil's favorite lies. He steadfastly insists that God *will not judge people*! Satan wanted Eve to know that God doesn't punish people. He wanted her (and everyone who would come after her) to reject the idea that God will hold people accountable for their sins. **He wanted her (and us) to have absolutely no fear of death, judgment or hell!**

Let's make a quick review. Here's the sequence Satan employs:

- Get people to *doubt* the inspiration, accuracy and authority of God's Word.

- Get people to *deny* the idea that God will judge anyone. In other words, get people to believe they are basically good and they are going to heaven because God is all-loving and all-forgiving.

When the devil accomplishes these two tasks, he literally flips the truth upside down. God (the *real* God) ceases to be acknowledged, and a new so-called God takes His place. This new made-up "God" punishes no one; there is no hell!

3. *He will try to convince you that God is a real killjoy and that you will find your deepest fulfillment when you think for yourself and do what <u>you</u> want to do.*

Satan said to Eve, *"God knows that your eyes will be opened as soon as you eat it, and you will be like God, knowing both good and evil."* TRANSLATION: "If you really want what is best in life, don't get tied down trying to obey all of God's ridiculous rules. You can do better than that. Make your own rules and find real happiness!"

Stated another way, Satan wants you to think that obeying God is for losers. If you really want to be fulfilled, follow your own dreams. Take off God's moral and spiritual straightjacket. Follow your own heart's desires. Set yourself free.

Literally billions of people around the entire globe have bought into these clever lies. They have cast off God's laws and decided to live by their own rules. And why have they done this? Because they have swallowed Satan's bait — hook, line an sinker!

- First, they *doubt* God's Word.
- Next, they *deny* God's Word.
- Finally, they *disobey* God's Word.

Remember it: *Doubt. Deny. Disobey.*

Let's wrap up this initial section. Satan is real, and he's out to ruin your life. But he won't approach you as the devil; he's too clever to make that mistake. Instead, he will wear a mask. His target will be your mind because he knows whoever controls you from the eyebrows up will also control you from your eyebrows down! His message will be subtle at first, then it will become more and more blatant. He wants you to doubt, deny and disobey God's Word. When that happens, he wins.

Don't permit the devil to trick and trap you. Believe God's Word A to Z. Follow it whole-heartedly.

Points to Ponder

1. What does it mean to say, "Satan wears a mask?"

2. Finish this quote: "Whoever controls you from your eyebrows up . . ." Illustrate what this means.

3. Identify and explain the devil's modus operandi.

4. Identify and explain the three main deceptions Satan wants to plant in your mind.

2
Satan's Helpers Wear Masks

Satan disguises himself as an angel of light.
So it is no wonder that <u>his servants also</u>
<u>disguise themselves</u> as servants of righteousness.
(1 Corinthians 11:14b-15a).

Tuck this truth deep inside your heart: *Satan doesn't work alone. He uses people, lots of people!*

The devil has a massive number of "servants" who work for him, and they also wear masks — masks of righteousness (imaginary innocence and goodness!). Outwardly, they seem to be as gentle and harmless as ordinary sheep, but inwardly (and almost always unknowingly) they are wolves who ensnare the hearts and minds of unsuspecting people. *They are soul killers! And unless you know how to recognize them, they will probably kill you!*

Here are some stunning facts from the Barna Research Group and LifeWay Research you need to examine closely. Take a deep breath and prepare yourself to be shocked.

- While about 70% of all the people in the United States classify themselves as Christians, only 7% of them actually possess a Bible-based faith! Let that number sink in: only 7%! **Most "believers" believe what is in their heart, not what is in the Bible!** It is no wonder Jesus said, *You can enter God's Kingdom only through the narrow gate. The highway to hell is broad, and its gate is wide for the many who choose that way. But the gateway to life is very narrow and the road is difficult, and <u>only a few ever find it</u>* (Matt. 7:13-14, NLT).

- Two-thirds of all Americans believe God accepts people from all religious backgrounds — even "good" atheists are thought to go to heaven. A huge 64% of all church goers agree with this statement! The Bible disagrees: *Salvation is found in no one else, for there is no other name under heaven given to mankind by which we must be saved (Acts 4:12).* That name is "Jesus."

- Sixty-seven percent of Catholics and fifty-five percent of Protestants believe a relationship with Jesus is *not* necessary in order to be forgiven or to go to heaven, even though Jesus said, **"I am the way, the truth and the life; <u>no one comes to the Father except through me</u>" (Jn. 14:6)!**

- Less than half of all professing Christians believe in a literal hell, in spite of the fact that Jesus explicitly mentioned it eleven times in his teachings!

- A mere 27% of Methodist pastors claim to get their core beliefs from the Scriptures. Similar small numbers can be found among the pastors in all of the mainline churches, such as the Episcopalian Church, the Presbyterian Church (USA), the Evangelical Lutheran Church and the United Church of Christ. The same weak percentages are present in the Catholic Church. Finally, just 15% of female pastors rely on the Bible as their primary guide for their beliefs. Generally, they are more "open minded" and liberal than their male counterparts.

I could go on and on, but I don't believe it is necessary. This is the bottom line: **Not everyone who claims to be a Christian is one! Satan has enlisted numerous sincere helpers (in churches, schools, universities, government, entertainment, sports and elsewhere) to twist the truth about God, the Bible, salvation, heaven and hell!**

Therefore, it is not surprising the Bible warns all of us to be on guard, because deception is far more prevalent than we think! Here are a few samples of the Bible ringing the alarm bells.

- *Beware of false prophets who come disguised as harmless sheep but are really vicious wolves (Matt. 7:15).*

- *"Not everyone who calls out to me, 'Lord! Lord!' will enter the Kingdom of Heaven. Only those who actually do the will of my Father in heaven will enter. On judgment day many will say to*

me, 'Lord! Lord! We prophesied in your name
and cast out demons in your name and per-
formed many miracles in your name.' But I will
reply, 'I never knew you. Get away from me, you
who break God's laws' (Matt. 7:21-23).

- But there were also false prophets in Israel, just
as there will be false teachers among you. They
will cleverly teach destructive heresies and even
deny the Master who bought them (2 Pet. 2:1a).

- Dear friends, I had been eagerly planning to
write to you about the salvation we all share.
But now I find that I must write about something else, urging you to defend the faith that
God has entrusted once for all time to his holy
people (Jude 1:3).

- I am shocked that you are turning away so soon
from God, who called you to himself through
the loving mercy of Christ. You are following a
different way that pretends to be the Good News
but is not the Good News at all. You are being
fooled by those who deliberately twist the truth
concerning Christ.

  Let God's curse fall on anyone, including us
  or even an angel from heaven, who preaches a
  different kind of Good News than the one we
  preached to you. I say again what we have said
  before: If anyone preaches any other Good News
  than the one you welcomed, let that person be
  cursed (Gal. 1:6-9).

Deception is a serious problem, and you must learn to recognize it! **Satan is real, and he wears a mask so you won't recognize him and his lies. Likewise, Satan's helpers also wear deceptive masks so they won't be easily spotted; they may seem to be sincere and good people, but upon closer inspection they prove to be dangerous phonies.**

Please believe me when I say, you can't identify imitation Christians by looking at their level of intelligence, sincerity or good deeds. You must dig deeper. For example, when I was in graduate school taking a class at an off-campus seminary, I studied under a highly esteemed professor. He taught us with remarkable skill and grace. Everyone liked him. But I sensed something was wrong. I couldn't identify the problem; so I met with him one-on-one. *It was then I learned this distinguished instructor didn't believe in the inspiration of the Bible, the reality of Satan, or the literal resurrection of Jesus Christ!* Every red flag and alarm went off! This Bible professor was a wolf in sheep's clothing!

In the rest of this book I want to show you how *you* can identify who is a *real* Christian!

Points to Ponder

1. What does it mean to say, "Satan's helpers wear masks?" Explain and illustrate your answer.

2. Identify the two most alarming facts you read from the Barna Group and LifeWay Research.

3. How seriously did the New Testament authors take the threat of deception? What is their advice in this matter?

4. Have you ever met a phony believer, including an imitation religious leader? Describe your experience.

Part Two
The Protection of Discernment

3

THE REAL CHRISTIAN NO LONGER FOLLOWS THE WORLD

One of my all-time favorite passages in the Bible is Ephesians 2:1-3. I have turned to this chapter and read these verses scores and scores of times. Why? Because they brilliantly describe a person's negative spiritual status before becoming a Christian, and because they explain the three things people do in order to receive this lethal status.

Let me ask you two all-important questions. *(1) Are you actually aware of how God views the majority of the people in the world right now? (2) Can you identify the three specific charges God has against everyone?* In other words, do you grasp how much danger most people are in, and do you fully understand why God is so upset with them?

Obviously, these are critical issues. Therefore, in this chapter, I want to help you see yourself as

God sees you (or as God *did* view you prior to becoming a Christian). Then, I will identify the three charges God has laid at the feet of everyone in the world. Let me begin by quoting Ephesians 2:1-3. Take some time to underline the key words and phrases in this passage.

> *As for you, you were dead in your transgressions and sins, in which you used to live when you followed the ways of this world and of the ruler of the kingdom of the air, the spirit who is now at work in those who are disobedient. All of us also lived among them at one time, gratifying the cravings of our flesh and following its desires and thoughts. Like the rest, we were by nature deserving of wrath.*

HOW GOD SEES US

First, I want you to notice how the Bible describes your past spiritual standing before God (and mine as well): *we were dead in our transgressions and sins!* Say it under your breath: "dead." You were *spiritually dead!* I was *spiritually dead!* God never says we were basically good or headed in the right direction. Instead, He says we were out of touch with Him, and we were in deep trouble!

You might say, "I never *felt* like I was doing something wrong; I never *imagined* I was guilty of sin." That's exactly what I told the police officer when I drove through a school zone too fast. I didn't know I was guilty; I didn't think I was speeding. But I *was* guilty; I *did* speed; even though I didn't realize it.

My wife, Carol, told me she never imagined she was guilty of sin until she realized there are two major categories of disobedience: sins of *commission* (doing those things that we know to be wrong) and sins of *omission* (failing to do the things we know we should do). For her, the sins of *omission* hit especially hard. She gave God little time or thought, expect on Sunday in church; the rest of the week she did whatever she wanted to do. It finally dawned on her that spiritual matters were not a priority in her life; she lived mostly for herself, not for God. She was guilty of putting God to the side while she pursued her own agenda. Let's take a closer look.

1. Guilty of Transgressions

The apostle Paul says we were all guilty of "transgressions and sins." By "transgressions" he is referring to those times when we cross the line and do things we know to be wrong. We do these wrong things in four areas of our life: in the *desires* of our heart, the *thoughts* of our mind, the *words* of our mouth and the *decisions* of our will. In all of these spheres we have committed transgressions of commission and omission — and we know it!

2. Guilty of Sins

When Paul states we are also guilty of "sins," he means we have all *fallen short of living up to God's standards.* We may be content with our own level of purity and spirituality, but God looks closer and says we should do better, much better.

A long time ago, Joy Dawson, a teacher at Youth With a Mission, explained to me that true obedience always has three characteristics: (1) it is prompt, (2) it is thorough, and (3) it is done with a positive attitude. If we fall short in any of these areas, then we are guilty of sin. The longer I thought about these criteria for obedience, the more clear it became that I have been guilty of sin countless times.

Here's the good news: the Bible says we "used" to live this way, and we "were" spiritually dead. Thankfully, that refers to our past, not to today. When we become true Christians, our past is completely forgiven! But before we discuss our conversion, let's examine the three reasons why we were in such deep trouble with God.

THREE SPECIFIC CHARGES AGAINST US

In Ephesians 2:1-3 we discover we were spiritually dead in our transgressions and sins for three specific reasons: we were guilty of inappropriate "following" — **we followed the world, the devil and our own sinful nature!** In the rest of this chapter we will examine our first major mistake: we "followed the world" — the secular culture (in following chapters we will investigate how we followed Satan and our sinful nature).

> *As for you, you were dead in your transgressions and sins, in which you used to live **when you followed the ways of this world** . . .*

In the past, prior to our conversion to Jesus Christ, we weren't interested in doing what *God* wanted, but in doing what *we* wanted. We looked like, sounded like, and behaved pretty much like everyone around us. We blended in. The world's possessions and pleasures were important to us — more important than finding and following God.

I will state it bluntly: we were distracted and deceived by the temptations that came to us from the world. We were guilty of loving the *creation* more than we cared about the wishes of the *Creator*. It's just that simple.

Try to imagine this scene from God's perspective. He is our heavenly Father; He created us to be part of His eternal Family; He loves us profoundly, and He simply wants us to love Him in return. But instead of caring about Him, there was a time when we primarily cared about everything else in the world. We didn't want to be guided by Him and His plans. We wanted one thing — our own way! And following that "way" (following that secular voice) of the world literally killed our relationship with God. Listen to the way the Bible describes our former addiction to the world and its fatal consequences.

> *Do not love the world or anything in the world. If anyone loves the world, love for the Father is not in them. For everything in the world — the lust of the flesh, the lust of the eyes, and the pride of life — comes not from the Father but from the world. The world and its desires pass away, but whoever does the will of God lives forever (1 Jn. 2:15-17).*

> *For the grace of God has appeared that offers salvation to all people. It teaches us to say "No"*

to ungodliness and worldly passions, and to live self-controlled, upright and godly lives in this present age, while we wait for the blessed hope—the appearing of the glory of our great God and Savior, Jesus Christ (Tit. 2:11-13).

Religion that God our Father accepts as pure and faultless is this: to look after orphans and widows in their distress and to keep oneself from being polluted by the world (Jas. 1:27).

You adulterous people, don't you know that friendship with the world means enmity against God? Therefore, anyone who chooses to be a friend of the world becomes an enemy of God (Jas. 4:4).

One of the ways you can spot a real Christian is by discovering what is most important to him. And you can be sure it won't be something on earth. He "used to" love and copy the world, but no longer. His views, values and vocabulary are not worldly any more, but spiritual. He marches to the beat of another drum. He lives by higher standards. He wants to please God in every area of his life. He follows God and the Bible, not the world!

Obviously, no one does this perfectly. *We all fall short of God's glorious standard (Rom. 3:23).* We all sin occasionally (1 Jn. 1:8-10). But the true believer is no longer dominated by sin. The Scriptures put it this way: *We know that anyone born of God does not continue to sin (1 Jn. 5:18a).* That is, he does not continue to live in sin as he had prior to his becoming a Christian. Now, he desires, for the first time, to please God. This is how you can discern the difference between a genuine and a counterfeit Christian — the real believer is not consumed with worldly interests, but with spiritual interests! The real believer lives to find and follow God's will!

Points to Ponder

1. Explain the spiritual status of everyone in the world before they become a true Christian. How does this reality apply to yourself?

2. What is the difference between sins of commission and sins of omission?

3. Every lost person is guilty of "transgressions." Explain what this means. Give examples.

4. Explain the meaning of "sin." Have you been guilty of this kind of disobedience? Explain.

5. What does it mean to be guilty of following the world? How do people do this today?

6. How can you identify a true Christian?

4

THE REAL CHRISTIAN NO LONGER FOLLOWS SATAN

> *As for you, you were dead in your transgressions and sins, in which you used to live **when you followed . . . the ruler of the kingdom of the air, the spirit who is now at work in those who are disobedient (Eph. 2:1-2).***

Have you ever taken a close look at world history? I was surprised to learn recently that scholars have found only eight years in all of history when there wasn't a war happening somewhere — *just eight years out of more than 6,000 years!* Then I checked to see how many battles the United States alone has been involved in during her short history. I was shocked. Wikipedia lists 120 battles we have participated in between 1775 and today! More than 1.3 million Americans have died, and another 1.5 million people have been wounded in these campaigns! Worst of all, we are no closer today than we were a thousand years ago in knowing how to end killing one another!

Of course, we could consider other alarming facts like these: (1) Out of the world's 9.8 million prisoners, nearly 25% of them (2.3 million) are located in the United States. (2) The American Addiction Center says 38% of all American adults struggle with an addiction. (3) An average of 20,000 people are murdered every year in the U.S. by fellow citizens. (4) There have been more than 61 million abortions (the taking of a baby's life!) since 1973 — that's an average of one killing every 96 seconds! (5) According to WatchBlog, federal, state and local governments spend around $280 billion annually on criminal justice! And these figures are just for the United States! They are as bad or worse elsewhere! Do you see a systemic problem here?

Honestly, why are there so many problems no one seems to know how to fix? What's wrong with us? **I'll tell you. We're in the mess we're in because we won't listen to God! A thousand men may hack at the branches of evil, but only one in that number will identify the root problems:** *we refuse to listen to God, but we are completely open to listening to the devil!* The Bible puts it this way: Before we become true Christians, we literally *followed the ruler of the kingdom of the air, the spirit who is now at work in those who are disobedient . . . we followed Satan!*

Here is a shocking mystery we must take seriously. We all imagine we are free to think for ourselves and to do for ourselves, but that simply isn't true! Before we turn to God in genuine repentance and faith, the spirit of Satan actually operates in our lives! Realize it or not, we have all been influenced by Satan and his demons; we have all been deceived and manipulated by him! This is one of three crucial facts that explain why our world is systemically corrupt: *(1) We follow the secular culture, (2) we follow the lying devil, and (3) we follow our own sinful natures.* Let's examine the second fatal flaw in this list. Slowly read through this short list and observe how Satan works in people right now:

1. When people hear the Biblical message about Jesus Christ and personal salvation, Satan is never far away. He literally approaches people and puts thoughts in their minds; he attempts to prevent them from believing God's Word, just as he did with Eve. *Some people are like seed along the path, where the word is sown. As soon as they hear it, Satan comes and takes away the word that was sown in them. (Mk. 4:15).* This explains why so many would-be followers of Christ simply don't complete the connection with God.

    The Bible gets even more explicit: *The god of this age has blinded the minds of unbelievers, so that they cannot see the light of the gospel that displays the glory of Christ, who is the image of God (2 Cor. 4:4; also see Acts 5:3 and Rev. 12:9).* People do not reject the gospel of Jesus Christ and salvation because it is unimportant or false; they reject it because they are duped by Satan!

2. The spirit of Satan deceives people so they will see everything from only a human perspective, rather than from a divine point of view. *When Jesus turned and looked at his*

disciples, he rebuked Peter. "Get behind me, Satan!" he said. "You do not have in mind the concerns of God, but merely human concerns" (Mk. 8:33). They devil doesn't want people to rely on the Bible and think the way God thinks; instead, he wants them to think without any input from God.

3. Satan literally works to oppose the spreading of the gospel of Jesus Christ and salvation. *We wanted to come to you . . . but Satan blocked our way (1 Thess. 2:18).* The last thing the devil wants to see is people becoming true Christians. Therefore, he will do everything he can to prevent the teaching of the Bible in nation after nation (especially in homes, churches and schools!).

4. In order to accomplish his purposes, Satan (or one of his demons) may even enter into people's bodies and control them! *Satan entered Judas, called Iscariot, one of the Twelve (Lk. 22:3; cf. Jn. 13:27). Jesus healed many who had various diseases. He also drove out many demons (Mk. 1:34).* The beliefs, behavior and illnesses of certain people defy normal explanations. Why? Because their beliefs, behaviors and illnesses are not normal; they are the by-product of demonic influence!

5. Satan also works tirelessly to tempt people with the practice of sexual immorality. *Do not deprive each other of sexual relations, unless you both agree to refrain from sexual intimacy for a limited time so you can give yourselves*

more completely to prayer. Afterward, you should come together again so that Satan won't be able to tempt you because of your lack of self-control (1 Cor. 7:5, NLT).

One morning the Lord showed me in a vision innumerable demons leaving Europe and entering both Canada and the United States. He said they would come and intensify sexual immorality in our two nations. Additionally, He explained how we had opened the door to them via our new liberal laws dealing with homosexuality. Since the time of that vision, our fall into sexual depravity has become unimaginable. What we once considered unthinkable, became tolerable, then acceptable, legal and even praised! Worse yet, those who condemn such sexual immorality are now said to be guilty of horrible hate crimes! What was once called "evil," is now called "good," and what was once considered "good," is now said to be "evil." With the devil's help, we have flipped sexual decency (and common sense) upside down (see Isa. 5:20)!

6. Satan hates Christianity because it exposes him and teaches the truth about God and salvation. Therefore, he creates numerous religions to compete with the one true faith. *What am I trying to say? Am I saying that food offered to idols has some significance, or that idols are real gods? No, not at all. I am saying that these sacrifices are offered to demons, not to God. And I don't want you to participate with*

demons (1 Cor. 10:19-20, NLT). While secular thinkers want people to tolerate (and even embrace) all of the world's religions, God exposes them for what they really are — false faiths headed by the devil!

7. The devil, the master mask wearer, raises up phony believers and places them in churches and Christian ministries (including seminaries!) in order to dilute and pollute the messages of the Bible. *These people are false apostles. They are deceitful workers who disguise themselves as apostles of Christ. But I am not surprised! Even Satan disguises himself as an angel of light. So it is no wonder that his servants also disguise themselves as servants of righteousness. In the end they will get the punishment their wicked deeds deserve (2 Cor. 11:13-15; also see Matt. 13:38-39; Rev. 2:24; 3:9).*

    Satan's "servants also disguise themselves." On the outside, they look perfectly normal, even religious, but on the inside they are empowered by Satan to keep people from taking God and His Word literally. The apostle Paul explains how you are to deal with these imitation spiritual leaders: *I am shocked that you are turning away so soon from God, who called you to himself through the loving mercy of Christ. You are following a different way that pretends to be the Good News but is not the Good News at all. You are being fooled by those who deliberately twist the truth concerning Christ.*

Let God's curse fall on anyone, including us or even an angel from heaven, who preaches a different kind of Good News than the one we preached to you. I say again what we have said before: If anyone preaches any other Good News than the one you welcomed, let that person be cursed (Gal. 1:6-9, NLT)! This warning was good in Paul's day, and it is equally relevant today as well. In fact, there is a high likelihood there are more than a couple fake churches and false religious leaders in your own community!

8. Most importantly, you need to know that the devil is a murderer; he kills people both physically and spiritually! *You belong to your father, the devil, and you want to carry out your father's desires. He was a murderer from the beginning, not holding to the truth, for there is no truth in him. When he lies, he speaks his native language, for he is a liar and the father of lies (Jn. 8:44).*

    Be alert and of sober mind. Your enemy the devil prowls around like a roaring lion looking for someone to devour (1 Pet. 5:8).

There is no end to the number of ways Satan advances his schemes in the world. Sometimes he is blatant in his activities — masterminding wars, espionage, injustice, drug distribution, sex trafficking, gang activities, and every other sort of corruption. Other times he is subtle, wearing a lovely mask — entertaining millions of people via television, movies, the internet, and sports. He works especially hard in religious groups in order to keep people from knowing God's Word and who are his very own masked children. Read carefully how the apostle John describes Satan's activities.

> *Dear children, don't let anyone deceive you about this: When people do what is right, it shows that they are righteous, even as Christ is righteous. But when people keep on sinning, it shows that they belong to the devil, who has been sinning since the beginning. But the Son of God came to destroy the works of the devil. Those who have been born into God's family do not make a practice of sinning, because God's life is in them. So they can't keep on sinning, because they are children of God. So now we can tell who are children of God and who are children of the devil. Anyone who does not live righteously and does not love other believers does not belong to God (1 Jn. 3:7-10, NLT).*

Let these works sink in deeply: *there are "children of God" and there are "children of the devil" throughout the world!* Every day, either in person or via some form of media, you see and hear these two sets of children. How do you know who's who? How can you distinguish between those who are real believers and those who wear masks? John answers that question. Children of God obey God, and children of the devil obey the devil. Real Christians are not perfect, but they do not make it a common practice to sin. They love God, and they desire to obey His Word.

Jesus told us how to detect phony people: **"By their fruit you will recognize them" (Matt. 7:16, 20).** In other words, look at the way people live. If someone truly believes and wants to follow God's Word, that person is the real deal. But someone denies God's Word or only gives it lip-service, then that person is a phony. Don't allow a person's sincerity or knowledge or popularity deceive you! Look deeper. Trust only those individuals who have a solid track record of living by the Bible, the whole Bible, and nothing but the Bible!

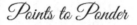

Points to Ponder

1. What's wrong with the world? Why is it in a constant state of chaos?

2. Identify two of the most prominent ways you witness Satan's involvement in people's lives.

3. What does it mean to say some people are "children of the devil?"

4. Based on this chapter, how would you identify a true Christian?

5
THE REAL CHRISTIAN NO LONGER FOLLOWS HIS SINFUL NATURE

> *As for you, you were dead in your transgressions and sins, in which you used to live when you followed the ways of this world and of the ruler of the kingdom of the air, the spirit who is now at work in those who are disobedient. **All of us also lived among them at one time, gratifying the cravings of our flesh and following its desires and thoughts. Like the rest, we were by nature deserving of wrath** (Eph. 2:1-3).*

It's a simple truth: before you can *defeat* a problem, you must first be able to *detect* it. This fact hit me especially hard recently. For three years I battled chronic breathing problems. I went to three different doctors, and they all tried to help me with one prescription after another. Finally, I went to an ear, nose and throat specialist. He identified the root cause in seconds: *I had polyps in my sinuses; I needed surgery.* Problem solved!

When you look at the world, it is obvious something is wrong — systemically wrong. But until you know how to *detect* the root causes behind these ailments, you will be hopeless in knowing how to *defeat* these problems. You may offer a million suggestions, like better education, more government involvement, improved distribution of wealth, higher levels of justice under the law, more high paying jobs, and so on. All of these ideas, and countless others like them, may contain a measure of relief, but none of them strike at the heart of the world's problems. This is where God and the Bible step up and offer us their insights. In Ephesians 2:1-3, we find heaven's explanation for earth's woes.

There are three all-critical crises in our world, and until you *detect* them, you will be helpless in knowing how to *defeat* them. The following insight from the Bible is important; notice how all three of our fundamental troubles are rooted in flawed people — people who have a "following" defect! They all unwisely follow . . .

1.   the secular lifestyle of the world
2.   the deceptive voice of Satan
3.   the desires of their own flesh (sinful nature).

So far in this book, we've examined the first two of these chronic defects in everyone. Now, we will examine the last one — the most difficult of the three ailments: our own sinful nature.

Here is a reality that almost no one accepts, but is, nevertheless, crucial to understanding human nature and the world's problems: *people, at their* *core, are <u>not</u> basically good, but inherently bad! Let me put it another way: we are all inclined to do whatever we want, without seeing the need to find and follow whatever God wants!* This is the way our pre-Christian personality works. We are hooked on being self-centered. The apostle Paul describes this condition perfectly:

> *I know that my selfish desires won't let me do anything that is good. Even when I want to do right, I cannot. Instead of doing what I know is right, I do wrong. And so, if I don't do what I know is right, I am no longer the one doing these evil things. The sin that lives in me is what does them.*
>
> *The Law has shown me that something in me keeps me from doing what I know is right. With my whole heart I agree with the Law of God. But in every part of me I discover something fighting against my mind, and it makes me a prisoner of sin that controls everything I do. What a miserable person I am. Who will rescue me from this body that is doomed to die* (Rom. 7:18-24, CEV).

Real Christians know better than anyone that they are their own worst enemy. They understand a reality few others are prepared to admit: *we are born sinners, not saints.*

One Sunday, an older lady came up to me after I preached a sermon on the depravity of our human nature. She was a visitor, and it was obvious she hadn't taken a bath for some time. She was dirty and carried an odor that easily resulted in social distancing. I was a little afraid she might want to give me a hug, but she didn't. All she wanted was to tell me one thing: *Pastor, I never met a person who gave me more trouble than myself!* With that, she turned and left. I never saw her again, but in that short moment she managed to say more in one sentence than I communicated in a full hour of preaching! *I never met a person who gave me more trouble than myself!*

Inside every human being — inside you and inside me! — there is a disposition that is damaged. We don't operate the way we were intended by God; we are warped; our desires, thoughts, speech and decisions are corrupted. We simply don't consistently do what we know we should do.

The prophet Jeremiah said it well: *The heart is deceitful above all things and beyond cure (17:9a).* This is a profound insight that we must memorize: *we deceive ourselves!* We think we know more than we do; we often imagine we even know more than God and His Book! And worst of all, the Bible says our corruption is *beyond cure;* it cannot be fixed by anything in this world!

If you can't trust your own heart, what are you supposed to do? Where can you turn? The answer is *upward* — *We can turn our hearts to God and ask Him to give us a new heart, a new disposition, a new nature.* And this is precisely what God does when we decide to stop following the world, the devil and our own twisted nature! Listen to what God says He will do for people who go to Him for help:

*This is the covenant I will establish with the
people of Israel after that time, declares the Lord.
I will put my laws in their minds and write
them on their hearts. I will be their God, and
they will be my people (Heb. 8:10; cf. 10:16).*

This promise is for both Jews and Gentiles.
Notice closely what it is God offers us: *We can get
a brand new heart and mind!* We can become new
people! The apostle Paul put it this way: *Anyone
who belongs to Christ has become a new person. The old
life is gone; a new life has begun (2 Cor. 5:17, NLT)!*

The systemic problems of the world are not
unfixable; they can be overcome, but only by God!
When a person comes to Him in the name of Jesus
Christ, when a person turns from his transgressions
and sins, when a person surrenders to God's Word,
at that moment a miracle happens. Now, for the
first time in his life, he can stop following the secular culture, the lies of Satan, and his own corrupt
nature. Now, he can go down a new path, a road
that leads to Divine forgiveness and supernatural
living! Take special notice of how the Scriptures
describe the presence and power of this new nature.
Take time to underline key words and phrases.

*Those who are dominated by the sinful
nature think about sinful things, but those who
are controlled by the Holy Spirit think about
things that please the Spirit. So letting your
sinful nature control your mind leads to death.
But letting the Spirit control your mind leads
to life and peace. For the sinful nature is always
hostile to God. It never did obey God's laws, and*

it never will. That's why those who are still under the control of their sinful nature can never
please God.

But you are not controlled by your sinful nature. You are controlled by the Spirit if
you have the Spirit of God living in you. (And
remember that those who do not have the Spirit
of Christ living in them do not belong to him at
all.) And Christ lives within you, so even though
your body will die because of sin, the Spirit gives
you life because you have been made right with
God. The Spirit of God, who raised Jesus from
the dead, lives in you. And just as God raised
Christ Jesus from the dead, he will give life to
your mortal bodies by this same Spirit living
within you.

Therefore, dear brothers and sisters, you
have no obligation to do what your sinful nature
urges you to do. For if you live by its dictates,
you will die. But if through the power of the
Spirit you put to death the deeds of your sinful
nature, you will live. For all who are led by the
Spirit of God are children of God (Rom. 8:5-14,
NLT).

With the Lord's authority I say this: Live no
longer as the Gentiles do, for they are hopelessly
confused. Their minds are full of darkness;
they wander far from the life God gives because
they have closed their minds and hardened their
hearts against him. They have no sense of shame.
They live for lustful pleasure and eagerly practice every kind of impurity.

But that isn't what you learned about
Christ. Since you have heard about Jesus and

have learned the truth that comes from him, throw off your old sinful nature and your former way of life, which is corrupted by lust and deception. Instead, let the Spirit renew your thoughts and attitudes. Put on your new nature, created to be like God—truly righteous and holy (Eph. 4:17-24, NLT).

Since you have been raised to new life with Christ, set your sights on the realities of heaven, where Christ sits in the place of honor at God's right hand. Think about the things of heaven, not the things of earth. For you died to this life, and your real life is hidden with Christ in God. And when Christ, who is your life, is revealed to the whole world, you will share in all his glory.

So put to death the sinful, earthly things lurking within you. Have nothing to do with sexual immorality, impurity, lust, and evil desires. Don't be greedy, for a greedy person is an idolater, worshiping the things of this world. Because of these sins, the anger of God is coming. You used to do these things when your life was still part of this world. But now is the time to get rid of anger, rage, malicious behavior, slander, and dirty language. Don't lie to each other, for you have stripped off your old sinful nature and all its wicked deeds. Put on your new nature, and be renewed as you learn to know your Creator and become like him. In this new life, it doesn't matter if you are a Jew or a Gentile, circumcised or uncircumcised, barbaric, uncivilized, slave, or free. Christ is all that matters, and he lives in all of us (Col. 3:1-11, NLT).

*No one who is born of God will continue to sin,
because God's seed remains in them; they cannot
go on sinning, because they have been born of
God. 10 This is how we know who the children
of God are and who the children of the devil are:
Anyone who does not do what is right is not
God's child, nor is anyone who does not love
their brother and sister (1 Jn. 3:9-10; also see
5:18-20).*

Let me urge you to read the above verses in
your own Bible. Study them deeply. Remind yourself of them often. Apply them continuously.

The real Christian, like everyone else in the
world, has a sinful nature. But he also has something that only Christians possess — he has a new
nature that can confront and conquer his old nature! Inside every true believer is the Holy Spirit,
and this Spirit teaches us how to master the desires
of our heart, the thoughts of our mind, the words of
our mouth, and the decisions of our will.

You can detect a real believer by his or her
power to change, to live a holy life. Phonies talk
the talk; genuine Christians walk the walk.

Points to Ponder

1. In your own words, explain the three rea-
    sons why the world is in such a mess.

2. Where you born with an innocent nature, or
    were you born with a sinful nature? Ex-

plain what this means and its implications for the rest of your life.

3. How does this sentence apply to you: *I never met a person who gave me more trouble than myself.*

4. What do Christians possess that no one else in the world possesses? How does this unique gift help them?

5. Based on this chapter, how can you identify a true Christian?

6
THE REAL CHRISTIAN IS BORN AGAIN

A very long time ago, when I was seventeen years old, I was hired to work as a teller in a large bank. I remember the day we were notified that someone in the area was using counterfeit money to make purchases; we were to be on the lookout for finding these fake bills.

As a busy teller, my hands would touch thousands of dollars every day, but I was a rookie, and my level of expertise was low. So I asked the head teller, "How can you identify a phony bill?" She responded confidently: "Once you become familiar enough with real money, you will almost always detect the imitation money as soon as you touch it." That simple explanation has stayed with me for more than fifty years: *I will be able to detect the counterfeit bills if I am well acquainted with the real ones.*

The same thing is true in the spiritual realm. *I will be able to detect fake a Christian because I know well the marks of a genuine believer.*

Why is this discernment important? Because if you listen to and believe the words of an imitation Christian (or any false teacher), you could end up following them all of the way to hell! I know that's strong wording, but listen to Jesus; he presents us with an identical dire warning:

> Woe to you, teachers of the law and Pharisees, you hypocrites! You shut the door of the kingdom of heaven in people's faces. You yourselves do not enter, nor will you let those enter who are trying to.
>
> Woe to you, teachers of the law and Pharisees, you hypocrites! You travel over land and sea to win a single convert, and when you have succeeded, you make them twice as much a child of hell as you are (Matt. 23:13-15).

OUCH! These are strong words, indeed! It *does* matter who you listen to; it *does* matter what you believe! Therefore, for your own spiritual safety you need to know whose teachings you can trust and whose views you should avoid! This single piece of advice could change your life for eternity!

THE INSIGHTFUL STORY
OF A RELIGIOUS SINNER

One night, under the cover of darkness, a man by the name of Nicodemus secretly approached Jesus. This was no average gentleman. He was a member of Israel's most devout religious body — the Pharisees. He would have been known far and wide as a man highly respected for meticulously keeping all 613 laws of God (plus many of the additional religious traditions). And he was more.

Nicodemus was also a member of Israel's Supreme Court (known as the Sanhedrin). This court of seventy-one judges oversaw both the religious and the social affairs of the Jewish people. In brief, Nicodemus was a high-ranking man in both the affairs of the *church* and the *state*. No one would dare to challenge his superlative credentials . . . but Jesus did that very thing!

The famous pastor and commentary writer, Matthew Henry, once said, *God not only sees me, He sees through me!* Jesus does the same thing; he sees through all of our church and worldly awards and titles; he sees what's actually inside our hearts!

When Jesus listened to Nicodemus, he didn't hear the voice of a prestigious leader. Instead, he looked beyond the trophies and honors this man could claim for himself. And when he did that, he saw a person who was spiritually lost! In spite of all his outward accomplishments, Jesus said this man was dead in his sins! Listen to Jesus' own words:

> *Very truly I tell you, no one can see the kingdom of God unless they are born again . . . You should not be surprised at my saying, 'You must be born again.' (Jn. 3:3, 7).*

Nicodemus was dumbfounded by Jesus' words! How could anyone dare to call a Pharisee and a

Sanhedrin judge a sinner who would not be part of God's eternal kingdom?! This was unthinkable, but Jesus wanted to make a point impeccably clear:

> *God doesn't save good people, power-ful people, popular people or even religious people! He only saves lost people — people who know they need His forgiveness!*

In the words of Jesus, Nicodemus needed to be "born again." This statement confused Nicodemus, and it continues to confuse many people today as well (including religious people!).

In the Greek language of the original New Testament, the word "again," carries two undisputed meanings: *again* and *above.* In other words, Nicodemus needed to be born again (a second time), but this time his birth must come from above (from God himself).

In our first birth, we are in debt to our physical parents for our new life. In our second birth, we owe God (Father, Son and Spirit) the credit for our spiritual restart.

The apostle Peter helps us here when he says this to his Christian audience: *You have been born again . . . through the living and enduring word of God (1 Pet. 1:23).* This sentence is very important because it explains how the people in Jesus' time were born again and how men, women, boys and girls can be born again today as well. If we will *listen* to God's Word in the Bible, *believe* God's Word, and *apply* God's Word to our lives, we will be born again!

God draws people to himself through preaching, teaching, witnessing and the simple sharing of God's Word with people. Listen to the way the apostle Paul makes this point. I want you draw a circle around these two key words: "ministry" and "message."

> *Therefore, if anyone is in Christ, the new creation has come: The old has gone, the new is here! All this is from God, who reconciled us to himself through Christ and gave us the ministry of reconciliation: that God was reconciling the world to himself in Christ, not counting people's sins against them. And he has committed to us the message of reconciliation. We are therefore Christ's ambassadors, as though God were making his appeal through us. We implore you on Christ's behalf: Be reconciled to God. God made him who had no sin to be sin for us, so that in him we might become the righteousness of God (2 Cor. 5:17-21, NIV).*

This is a mouth-full. Let me break it down into bite-size portions.

First, when you become a true Christian, you are transformed into a new person! You change. Your desires, thoughts, speech and decisions are impacted. Now, for real, you want to please God!

Second, when you become a real believer, you know you have been reconciled to God through the work of Jesus Christ dying on the cross for your sins. You didn't become a Christian by any merits on your part, but solely on the merits of Christ which were applied to your heart.

Third, when you become an authentic Christian, as a result of this new birth, wherever you go, you now become one of God's ambassadors. And through you, as you speak God's Word to people, they can be born again! **This is *your* "ministry" and "message."**

Every true Christian has had the "born again" experience, not because they are good people, but because they believed God's message to them; they trusted God's Word, and they accepted the teachings of the Bible about sin, repentance and forgiveness!

Now, I want to finish the story about Nicodemus; he appears in John's Gospel two more times.

In his second appearance, we see him in a meeting with the Sanhedrin. All of the judges in this court are criticizing Jesus and wanting to condemn him, but Nicodemus speaks up and tells everyone not to be so quick to pass judgment. He is mocked for his defense of Jesus (Jn. 7:25-52).

Finally, we observe Nicodemus one more time. On this occasion, Jesus has been crucified and a secret disciple by the name of Joseph has gotten permission to place the battered body in his own tomb. Assisting him in this task was Nicodemus, who brought seventy-five pounds of spices in order to give Jesus a proper burial! He is no longer hiding in the dark; instead, he is unashamedly displaying his allegiance to Jesus in the full light of the day! He has become a true follower of Jesus (Jn. 19:38-40). He has been "born again," and no one could deny it!

Points to Ponder

1. If Nicodemus wasn't saved, in spite of all his credentials, how does that fact impact the way you think of religious leaders and even yourself?

2. What does it mean to say, "God doesn't save good people."

3. In your own words, explain Jesus' saying, "You must be born again."

4. What instrument does God use to bring about a person's spiritual birth. Illustrate how this works. Is this the way you became "born again?" Explain.

5. How well do you know the "message" of reconciliation? God sees you as a "minister" of that "message." Do you view yourself as one of God's ministers/ambassadors? Are you asking the Lord to use you this way?

7
THE REAL CHRISTIAN HAS A TESTIMONY

Recently, I spoke with a young man who told me he was a Christian. I wanted to rejoice with him, but I had my doubts (not about his sincerity, but his actual conversion to Christ). So I asked him to share with me his *testimony*. I wanted to know when, where and how he became a follower of Jesus.

No one is *born* a Christian. True believers are *born again*. So, I wanted to hear this person's story. It isn't rude to ask someone to tell you their testimony; for real Christians, it's an honor to share with people what Jesus Christ has done for them!

The apostle Paul is a good example in this regard. He told his testimony, in part or in whole, no less than six times in the New Testament. Let me show you his basic outline (an outline you can easily apply to your own story).

1. His Past

Paul begins his testimony with an acknowledgement of his sinful past. He wasn't proud of his ignorance and actions before his conversion. In fact, in great humility, Paul was always quick to describe himself as wholly unworthy of the gift of salvation. Here are his own words:

> *This is a trustworthy saying, and everyone should accept it: "Christ Jesus came into the world to save sinners" —and I am the worst of them all" (1 Tim. 1:16, NLT).*

Paul never let anyone think he was born again because of something he did to deserve it. To the contrary, he went the second mile to make it impeccably clear that his salvation was completely an act of grace (God's supernatural and undeserved help).

Paul would tell people how sinful he was in his past because he wanted everyone hearing him to know that no one was beyond the reach of God's love and forgiveness. This was his reasoning: "If God could save Paul, then God could save anyone!" Paul stated it this way: *God had mercy on me so that Christ Jesus could use me as a prime example of his great patience with even the worst sinners. Then others will realize that they, too, can believe in him and receive eternal life (1 Tim. 1:17).*

Real Christians feel the same way Paul felt — unworthy and humbled by the thought that Jesus would leave heaven, come to earth, and die on the cross to pay the price for their own sins! Personally, I had no interest in the things pertaining to God prior to my own conversion. When I think back on my life prior to my conversion, I often shake my head and often expel an involuntary grunt of disgust at my foolish pride and lifestyle. I *know* my salvation had nothing to do with my goodness, but wholly to do with God's own goodness!

2. His Conversion

In every testimony there needs to be a recounting of where and when you crossed the line from sinner to believer. For some people, this event may have been easy and not dramatic. But for others, like Paul, it was a substantial and unforgettable experience. Here is his own story.

> *"I am a Jew, born in Tarsus of Cilicia, but brought up in this city. I studied under Gamaliel and was thoroughly trained in the law of our ancestors. I was just as zealous for God as any of you are today. I persecuted the followers of this Way to their death, arresting both men and women and throwing them into prison, as the high priest and all the Council can themselves testify. I even obtained letters from them to their associates in Damascus, and went there to bring these people as prisoners to Jerusalem to be punished.*
>
> *"About noon as I came near Damascus, suddenly a bright light from heaven flashed around me. I fell to the ground and heard a voice say to me, 'Saul! Saul! Why do you persecute me?'*
>
> *"'Who are you, Lord?' I asked.*
>
> *" 'I am Jesus of Nazareth, whom you are persecuting,' he replied. My companions saw the light, but they did not understand the voice of*

him who was speaking to me.
"'What shall I do, Lord?' I asked.
" 'Get up,' the Lord said, 'and go into Da-
mascus. There you will be told all that you have
been assigned to do' (Acts 22:3-10).

Paul gave this testimony to the Jewish people, to the governor Felix, to his successor, Festus, and to King Agrippa (Acts 9, 24-26). It is likely he gave it again before the Emperor in Rome.

Paul's conversion to Christ marked a turning point in his life. He could look back to this day and this experience as a special marker, a time when he turned from self-centeredness to Christ-centeredness. Before his encounter with Jesus, he followed his own agenda without any hesitation or guilt. But when he met Jesus, his life took on a new direction and meaning. From this time onward, he would gladly seek to find and follow His plans, not his own!

The same thing happened to me. I was on track to become a CPA (certified public accountant) and a bank officer. But when I asked Jesus for the forgiveness of my sins, I got that *and much more!* For the very first time in my life I hungered to know God and His will better and better. Church, which previously meant nothing to me, now was a place I loved; I attended every meeting (three times a week). My life would never be the same. As a college student, I changed my major from Accounting to Biblical Studies. My priorities, values and lifestyle were all deeply impacted. I was a new person!

3. His New Life in Christ

In Paul's testimony, he did more than point to the past. He made it plain that his whole life would now be focused on living for Christ. Jesus, for Paul, would be both his moment-by-moment Boss and his Best Friend! Here are his own words.

> *I have been crucified with Christ and I no longer live, but Christ lives in me. The life I now live in the body, I live by faith in the Son of God, who loved me and gave himself for me (Gal. 2:20).*

> *As for me, may I never boast about anything except the cross of our Lord Jesus Christ. Because of that cross, my interest in this world has been crucified, and the world's interest in me has also died (Gal. 6:14, NLT).*

> *For to me, living means living for Christ, and dying is even better (Phil. 1:21).*

When Paul became a Christian, his old life died; he would from that moment forward dedicate his entire life to pleasing God! He would not have a "Sunday" faith or a "moral" faith or a do-good-deeds faith. Instead, he would have a faith that essentially said, "I surrender. My life is Yours. Use me however it pleases You. I will hold back nothing."

I will never compare my own life with Paul's example. He will win that comparison every time. But I can honestly say, my life is grounded in the holy Trinity (God the Father, God the Son, and God the Spirit) and in the Bible. Every morning, with very few exceptions, I lift my hands to God Almighty and say, "Lord, help me find and follow the center of Your will today!" My constant aim is to be close to Him, to hear His voice, and to do whatever He wants me to do. That, my friend, is the way you can identify a real Christian — he or she has a personal testimony. They can say, with the lyrics of "Amazing Grace," *I once was lost, but now am found!*

Understand, real Christians are more than "good" or "sincere" people; they are "spiritual" at their core. They take God and His Word seriously. They are obedient the majority of the time. Listen to the way the apostle John describes the life of the genuine believer.

We know that God's children do not make a practice of sinning (1 Jn. 5:18a, NLT).

Dear children, don't let anyone deceive you about this: When people do what is right, it shows that they are righteous, even as Christ is righteous. But when people keep on sinning, it shows that they belong to the devil, who has been sinning since the beginning. But the Son of God came to destroy the works of the devil. Those who have been born into God's family do not make a practice of sinning, because God's life is in them. So they can't keep on sinning, because they are children of God. So now we can tell who are children of God and who are children of the devil. Anyone who does not live righteously and does not love other believers does not belong to God (1 Jn. 3:7-10, NLT).

There are no perfect Christians — you will never find one. But when you find a real believer, you can be certain of two things: (1) they will have a born again experience, and (2) they will have a personal testimony.

Points to Ponder

In the space below, write out your own personal testimony.

My Past

My Conversion

My New Life in Christ

ADDITIONAL RESOURCES TO HELP YOU GROW
Available from www.Making Disciples.US

Go to my website and get a FREE book of your choice!

- *Essentials for Living the Christian Life*

- *Amazing Truths*

- *My Personal Journey with God*

- *Great Daily Devotions*

- *Sixteen Ways to Read the Bible*

- *Miracles are Real*

- *From Eternity to Eternity*

- *5 Reasons Why You Can Trust the Bible*

- *Spiritual Development*

- *Thinking Biblically 1 and 2*

- *The Core Twelve Beliefs*

- *When Life Flips Upside Down*

- *The Only Way to Heaven — Really!*

And more.

About the Author

Stephen Swihart has been married to Carol for over fifty years. They have two grown children and five grandchildren. Their greatest joy is to know their children and grandchildren are walking in the Lord's truth!

For twenty years Steve served as a pastor. For the next nearly ten years he was a Bible professor and Graduate Dean. After this he has spent all of his time in writing, mentoring (intentional discipleship) and speaking. He earned his Master and Doctorate degrees from Ashland Theological Seminary in Ashland, Ohio.

Made in the USA
Monee, IL
17 January 2021